George Washington Ranck

O'Hara and His Elegies

George Washington Ranck

O'Hara and His Elegies

ISBN/EAN: 9783744652711

Printed in Europe, USA, Canada, Australia, Japan

Cover: Foto ©Thomas Meinert / pixelio.de

More available books at **www.hansebooks.com**

O'Hara and His Elegies.

BY

GEORGE W. RANCK,

BALTIMORE:
TURNBULL BROTHERS.
1875.

TO ONE

𝔚𝔥𝔬𝔰𝔢 𝔏𝔦𝔣𝔢 𝔴𝔞𝔰 𝔞 𝔓𝔬𝔢𝔪

THIS LITTLE BOOK

IS INSCRIBED.

.

Lexington, Ky., 1875.

EXTRACT FROM LETTER.

NEAR FRANKFORT, KY., *August 15th*, 1875.

MR. G. W. RANCK,

Dear Friend: *   *   *   *   *   *   *   *   *

And in conclusion I have one request to make. When you publish your tribute to my brother Theodore, say that it is accompanied not only by the entire endorsement of his family, but by their warmest gratitude and love; for you have done more than all others to cause his poems to be properly appreciated, and you of all the world moved his fellow-citizens to that sacred act — the bringing home of those dear remains. You will comply with my request, for it is a sacred one, and besides you would not have us to appear ungrateful.

As ever, your friend,

MARY O'HARA PRICE.

INDEX.

THE BIVOUAC OF THE DEAD.

——•——

THE muffled drum's sad roll has beat
    The soldier's last tattoo ;
No more on life's parade shall meet
    The brave and daring few.
On Fame's eternal camping-ground
    Their silent tents are spread,
And Glory guards with solemn round
    The bivouac of the dead.

No answer of the foe's advance

Now swells upon the wind ;

No troubled thought at midnight haunts

Of loved ones left behind ;

No vision of the morrow's strife

The warrior's dream alarms ;   .

No braying horn nor screaming fife

At dawn shall call to arms.

Their shivered swords are red with rust ;

Their plumèd heads are bowed ;

Their haughty banner, trailed in dust,

Is now their martial shroud ;

And plenteous funeral-tears have washed

The red stains from each brow,

And their proud forms, in battle gashed,

Are free from anguish now.

The neighing steed, the flashing blade,

    The trumpet's stirring blast,

The charge, the dreadful cannonade,

    The din and shout, are past ;

No war's wild note, nor glory's peal,

    Shall thrill with fierce delight

Those breasts that nevermore shall feel

    The rapture of the fight.

Like the dread northern hurricane

    That sweeps his broad plateau,

Flushed with the triumph yet to gain,

    Came down the serried foe.

Our heroes felt the shock, and leapt

    To meet them on the plain;

And long the pitying sky hath wept

    Above our gallant slain.

Sons of our consecrated ground,

   Ye must not slumber there,

Where stranger steps and tongues resound

   Along the heedless air.

Your own proud land's heroic soil

   Shall be your fitter grave :

She claims from war his richest spoil —

   The ashes of her brave.

So 'neath their parent turf they rest,

   Far from the gory field ;

Borne to a Spartan mother's breast

   On many a bloody shield.

The sunshine of their native sky

   Smiles sadly on them here,

And kindred hearts and eyes watch by

   The heroes' sepulchre.

Rest on, embalmed and sainted dead !

    Dear as the blood you gave,

No impious footsteps here shall tread

    The herbage of your grave ;

Nor shall your glory be forgot

    While fame her record keeps,

Or honor points the hallowed spot

    Where valor proudly sleeps.

Yon marble minstrel's voiceless tone

    In deathless songs shall tell,

When many a vanquished age hath flown,

    The story how ye fell.

Nor wreck, nor change, or winter's blight,

    Nor time's remorseless doom,

Shall dim one ray of holy light

    That gilds your glorious tomb.

THE OLD PIONEER.

A DIRGE for the brave old pioneer!
    Knight-errant of the wood!
Calmly beneath the green sod here
    He rests from field and flood ;
The war-whoop and the panther's screams
    No more his soul shall rouse,
For well the aged hunter dreams
    Beside his good old spouse.

A dirge for the brave old pioneer !

  Hushed now his rifle's peal ;

The dews of many a vanish'd year

  Are on his rusted steel ;

His horn and pouch lie moldering

  Upon the cabin-door ;

The elk rests by the salted spring,

  Nor flees the fierce wild boar.

A dirge for the brave old pioneer !

  Old Druid of the West !

His offering was the fleet wild deer,

  His shrine the mountain's crest.

Within his wildwood temple's space

  An empire's towers nod,

Where erst, alone of all his race,

  He knelt to Nature's God.

A dirge for the brave old pioneer !

Columbus of the land !

Who guided freedom's proud career

Beyond the conquer'd strand ;

And gave her pilgrim sons a home

No monarch's step profanes,   .

Free as the chainless winds that roam

Upon its boundless plains.

A dirge for the brave old pioneer !

The muffled drum resound !

A warrior is slumb'ring here

Beneath his battle-ground.

For not alone with beast of prey

The bloody strife he waged,

Foremost where'er the deadly fray

Of savage combat raged.

A dirge for the brave old pioneer!

A dirge for his old spouse!

For her who blest his forest cheer,

And kept his birchen house.

Now soundly by her chieftain may

The brave old dame sleep on,

The red man's step is far away,

The wolf's dread howl is gone.

A dirge for the brave old pioneer!

His pilgrimage is done;

He hunts no more the grizzly bear

About the setting sun.

Weary at last of chase and life,

He laid him here to rest,

Nor recks he now what sport or strife

Would tempt him further west.

A dirge for the brave old pioneer !

The patriarch of his tribe !

He sleeps — no pompous pile marks where,

No lines his deeds describe.

They raised no stone above him here,

Nor carved his deathless name — .

An empire is his sepulchre,

His epitaph is Fame.

NOTE.— The last stanza of this ode was written before Boone's monument had been erected.

O'HARA AND HIS ELEGIES.

By George W. Ranck.

———•———

A MERICA has as yet produced but one elegiac poet
of acknowledged genius, and that poet is Theodore
O'Hara, author of "The Bivouac of the Dead" and the
ode to Daniel Boone. The remarkable merit of these
tender, mournful, but inspiring elegies has never been
disputed. They have always been most warmly admired
by the scholarly and the cultivated; have grown steadily
in public estimation from the time they were penned, and
will continue to grow in favor with the growth of years.
May we not reasonably hazard the prophecy that the time

will come when O'Hara will occupy the same place in our
literature that is now held in the field of English letters
by the celebrated author of the " Elegy in a Country
Churchyard "?   Feeling that Americans should know more
of the gifted man whose poems have reflected honor upon
them, and with the hope of increasing the number of
his admirers, the writer resolved to publish this little
volume.   The facts of the life of O'Hara were obtained
from papers and documents placed in the hands of the
writer by the family of the poet, and also from letters received from his old comrades and intimate friends.

Theodore O'Hara was born in Danville, Kentucky,
February 11th, 1820.   He was the son of Kane O'Hara,
an Irish political exile, noted for his piety and learning,
who had been invited to Danville to take charge of an
academy about to be established there under the auspices
of Governor Shelby.   His ancestors becoming subjected
to the disabilities imposed upon Catholics in their unhappy
land, abandoned home rather than religion, emigrated

to this country with Lord Baltimore, and aided in founding that colony which was so long an asylum for victims of religious intolerance. The family removed from Danville to Woodford County, where the father himself commenced the education of his son. They subsequently settled in Frankfort, where several members of the family still reside.

Theodore O'Hara was remarkable when but a child. Study was his passion. It engrossed his entire boyhood, and added fuel to the fires of his genius. Happily, he was trained and appreciated by one who fully understood the nature he was moulding. His education was conducted wholly by his father until he was prepared to enter college, and then that ripe scholar had so thoroughly done his work that he was at once admitted to the senior class of St. Joseph's Academy at Bardstown. There, among the learned clergy of his church, he soon became preeminent as a profound and accomplished scholar, especially in the ancient classics ; and though but a youth, the rare compliment was paid him of election to the professorship of the Greek language. He bade farewell to his Alma Mater on graduating, in a speech so full of eloquence as never to be forgotten by those who listened enraptured to it. One has said of it—"It was the most perfect address I ever heard for elegance of style, depth of thought, truthfulness of sentiment, and beauty of composition." After leaving college he studied law in the office of Judge Owsley, where he was a fellow-student of Gen. John C. Breckinridge, and the strong attachment there formed between the young men lasted through all his subsequent life. In 1845 he held a position in the Treasury Department at Washington, under Gen. John M. McCalla, but his life from this time till its close was obscured by the same dark clouds of misfortune and disappointment that seem so strangely to hang round the pathway of genius— the pressure of a narrow fortune combined with the aspiration of a noble ambition conspired to make his life erratic. He was appointed to a captaincy in the "old" United States Army when such a position was a sure indication of merit, served with distinction through the Mexican War, and was breveted Major for gallant and meritorious conduct. Contrary to modern usage, he left the army at the close of the war, enriched only in reputation, and immediately commenced the practice of law in Washington City, where he remained until the breaking out of the Cuban fever, when, with many other gallant Kentuckians, he embarked in that ill-fated enterprise. He commanded one of the regiments in the disastrous battle of Cardenas, and was badly wounded.

During the absence of the Hon. John Forsythe as minister to Mexico, Col. O'Hara conducted the *Mobile Register* as editor-in-chief, with signal ability and success ; in fact he was peculiarly fitted for an editor, as his knowledge was varied, deep and comprehensive, and the glowing sentences flashed like jewels from his gifted pen. He was subsequently editor of the *Louisville Times*, and afterwards of the *Frankfort Yeoman*. He was frequently called on by the Government to conduct diplomatic negotiations of importance with foreign nations, and his services were specially valued in the Tehauntepec-Grant business. In 1854, when the remains of the distinguished statesman, Hon. William T. Barry, arrived from Liverpool and were re-interred in the State Cemetery at Frankfort, Col. O'Hara was the orator of the occasion, and delivered an oration so glowing, so chaste and appropriate, and so full of pure and lofty eloquence, as to entitle it to a place among the best specimens of American oratory.

At the beginning of the late war his heart swelled with sympathy for the people he had always loved so well, and his sword was at once unsheathed in defence of the South. He was immediately honored with an important position, and soon promoted to the colonelcy of the Twelfth Alabama regiment. He subsequently served on the staff of that lamented hero, Gen. Albert Sidney Johnston, stemmed with him the fiery flood of Shiloh, and received his great chief in his arms when he fell upon that ensanguined field. He was also chief of staff to Gen. John C. Breckinridge ;

and true to the last to his old friend, he shared with him all the bitterness of the last bitter days, when one of the grandest dreams of modern times dissolved and ended, and never left him till he saw him safely embarked for a foreign shore. The close of this war also found him without a dollar, but like thousands of his comrades, he went at once to work to retrieve his fortunes. He went to Columbus, Georgia, and engaged in the cotton business with a relative; but misfortune again overtook him, for he and his partner lost all by fire. Undismayed, he retired to a plantation on the Alabama side of the Chattahoochie, near a place called Guerrytown, and there he was laboring successfully when he was attacked with bilious fever, of which he died Friday, June 6, 1867. His latest hours were cheered by the affectionate attentions of devoted relatives and friends. He received the sacraments of his church from the hands of a pious clergyman ; and as the soft Southern breeze bore to him the songs of birds and the odor of sweet flowers, the soldier-poet fell asleep calmly, hopefully and resigned. His remains were taken from Barbour County, Alabama, to Columbus, Georgia, and there buried in consecrated ground, where he slept until the State upon which his genius had been reflected proudly claimed his ashes. In the summer of 1874, in accordance with a resolution of the Kentucky Legislature, all that was mortal of the poet was brought to Frankfort; and on the 15th of September of that year, his remains, together with those of Governors Greenup and Madison, and several distinguished officers of the Mexican War, were re-interred with appropriate ceremonies in the State Cemetery. The last tribute was paid by mourning relatives and friends, by old comrades and State troops, by the Governor of the Commonwealth, the heads of departments and a throng of sorrowing admirers. The solemn boom of the minute-gun, and the " sad roll " of the " muffled drum," mingled with his funeral dirge, and the shadow of the tattered banner under which he had fought on " Angustura's bloody plains " rested silently and lovingly upon his bier. O'Hara was

buried in the military lot on the east side of the monument to the soldiers whose dirge he had so eloquently
sung, and midway between that stately pile and the tomb
of the vanquisher of Tecumseh. His grave was wreathed
with evergreens and strewn with flowers, and over it the
attendant companies of the State Guard fired three volleys
of musketry. After the last sad rites had been performed,
and during the delivery of the funeral oration, Gen.
William Preston, of Lexington, Kentucky, said of O'Hara :
" Having known Col. O'Hara intimately, both in his cam-
paigns in Mexico and in the South ; having enjoyed the
pleasures that his cultivated mind and genial temper gave
to the camp-fire or the march ; having witnessed his
brilliant courage and quick discernment in battle ; having
seen him in the defiles of Mexico, by the side of Sidney
Johnston in his dying moments at Shiloh, and with Breckinridge in his charge at Stone River ; I here, in this
solemn moment, can sincerely say that I believe no
braver heart will rest beneath this consecrated sod, and

no spirit more knightly or humane ever lingered under the shadow of yonder monument." The obsequies closed with the reading of " The Bivouac of the Dead " by Henry T. Stanton, who prefaced the reading with the apposite remark that " O'Hara, in giving utterance to this song, became at once the builder of his own monument and the author of his own epitaph." It was meet and well that a Kentucky soldier and a Kentucky poet should mingle the laurel with the cypress at the grave of the immortal soldier-poet of Kentucky.

O'Hara was never married. In personal appearance he was strikingly handsome. He was not quite six feet in height, very graceful and erect in his carriage, and scrupulously neat in his dress. His face beamed with generous feeling; his dark hazel eyes kindled with soul and expression, and "were filled with a light like that which comes down to us from the stars." His whole personnel indicated a refinement that sat upon him like a birthright. Another has said of him :—" His soul was all chivalry and honor, his heart all aglow with generous impulse, and his brain trained by discipline and stored with rich and varied learning. To his friends his society was a continual feast, where his solid acquirements were garnished with the graces of true poetry and the delicacy of true wit. He was indeed a charming companion. True and unselfish, talented and brave ; tried by adversity and prosperity, yet ever found unfaltering in his honor, he is gone crowned with the commendations of all who knew him." O'Hara was indeed tried by adversity, and his great heart and refined nature made him doubly susceptible of the pain and suffering that the vicissitudes of life heaped upon him. Like Chatterton, he tasted the dregs of a bitter cup ; but unlike that marvellous but ill-fated genius, he met his trials like a brave man and died with his armor on.

The political essays, public addresses and literary compositions of O'Hara would fill a volume, for he was a ready and prolific writer; but his fame rests upon his elegies. It is as a poet that O'Hara is known and celebrated; and who will deny him that exalted name after reading his inspired verses? That one great lyric, " The Bivouac of the Dead," would alone have made his name immortal. It is his masterpiece. As '' The Raven " stands apart and above all the writings of Poe, so is this poem, compared with all that O'Hara ever wrote. It was written in August, 1847, for the dedication of the chaste and beautiful military monument erected in the State Cemetery at Frankfort, to the memory of the gallant Kentuckians who fell in the Mexican War. Col. O'Hara was at that time editor of the *Frankfort Yeoman*. This poem has all the mournful melody which belongs to that sad and beautiful requiem, by the unfortunate William Collins, entitled '' How Sleep the Brave," while as a martial elegy it even surpasses the famous stanzas by Charles Wolfe on " The Burial of Sir John Moore." The artistic execution of this ode is almost faultless ; but it is when we look at it in the light of those higher qualities which constitute the excellence of all true poetry that we fully comprehend its merit and power. In the perfect harmony of the spirit and tone of his verse with his theme ; in the perfect adaptation of his style to his subject, and in the moving and solemn accord of the measure of his own spirit with that of his verse, these lines of O'Hara are unsurpassed. The soul of the writer moves and sings with the soul of his subject. Indeed, he times his verse not only to the martial measure, but to the solemn spirit-tread with which we would imagine his fellow-heroes to march "o'er Fame's eternal camping-ground." The heroic yet mournful and mysterious beating of the feet of the song seems the same as that of "glory," as " with solemn round " she " guards "—

" The bivouac of the dead."

In this perfect harmony of spirit, style and subject, and in this tuneful accord of the spirit of the writer with that of his theme, this piece is fully equal to Longfellow's " Psalm of Life." But there is a second quality in which it far

surpasses that moral-heroic production, and it consists in
that power peculiar to some poets of reaching out and
touching the borders of the unseen. This quality is developed by Longfellow in those more than beautiful lines
" The Footsteps of the Angels ;" but in this O'Hara far
transcends him. Longfellow invites the dwellers of the
spirit-realm into our homes and " lays their angel hands in
ours ;" but moved by the breath of eternal song, the blos-
soms of O'Hara's soul not only bend and blow toward that
mystic and shadowy land, but he visits himself the dwell-
ing-place of spirits, lives and moves among their shining
legions, and opens to us the gates of the unseen world, that
we too may look again upon those once familiar " proud
forms " and " plumed heads." This is the difference which
exists between the heroic and the tender, and this gives to
" The Bivouac of the Dead " its solemn majesty and sub-
lime beauty. This poem possesses a touch of another
quality which gives to poetry its loftiest elevation. It is
not outwardly developed by any word or figure, but in the

first few stanzas of the ode a sympathetic reader will find himself inhaling that peculiar, sad and solemn atmosphere of prophecy which most strangely and mournfully hangs about the spirits of some of the gifted of earth. The nature of the soul and song of the writer seems to be attuned so exactly to that of the departed heroes of whom he sings, that behind the martial measure of his verse there seems to move a muffled fate which whispers that their home will soon be his. The combination which this production contains of spirit-reach and spirit-prescience is the highest, strangest and most solemn gift a poet may possess. Genius has truly breathed immortal life into these lines, and they will live when many of the fading, dying things that now are seen in American literature shall have passed away forever. If it had no other claim upon life than the sublimely beautiful metaphor in the first stanza, that alone would preserve it through the ages. Where, in the English language, is there a bolder, grander or loftier conception than that in which our departed heroes are represented as encamped on the vast and illimitable plains of immortality, while the guardian spirit of the mighty host watches with ceaseless and untiring vigilance over the shadowy inhabitants of those silent tents? The hold of this elegy upon the popular heart grows stronger and more enduring. It is creeping into every scrap-book ; it is continually quoted upon public occasions. Every year or two it makes the round of the American press, and recently it has excited enthusiastic admiration in England. One stanza of it was inscribed upon a rude memorial nailed to a tree upon the battle-field of Chancellorsville ; another was engraved upon a military monument at Boston, Mass., and still another adorns a memorial column that marks the place where occurred one of the most bloody contests of the Crimean war. It will gain the high place in literature that it merits, and there it will remain.

Next to his masterpiece comes the simple but noble tribute penned by O'Hara at the grave of Daniel Boone.

These are the only verses the writer has ever seen that did justice to the "old Druid of the West," and we love the brave hunter more than ever, and appreciate his big honest heart, his undaunted spirit, and the grandeur of his mission tenfold more after reading them. In Canto VIII. of *Don Juan* Byron introduces a number of stanzas descriptive of Boone and his backwoods life ; but with all his poetic power, even the bard of Newstead Abbey, on this field at least, must lower his plume to O'Hara. It is true that both the measure and the style of the stanzas com- pared are different ; but in that which both attempt — a de- lineation of the simple rugged nature of the man and his wildwood home, Lord Byron has not met with the success of O'Hara. The sad notes of this sweet and solemn dirge will float and linger with undying cadence for generations to come, around the name of Daniel Boone, " the Columbus of the land,"

" Who guided freedom's proud career
 Beyond the conquered strand."

His deeds, his frank and honest character, his fearless heart and romantic and providential life, cannot be forgotten while these stanzas live. The children of our children's children will read them, and see in fancy

> "His horn and pouch lie moldering
> Upon the cabin door,"

and will realise that the conqueror of the wilderness

> "Hunts no more the grizzly bear
> About the setting sun."

But this poem is not only a tender dirge, it is an elevated, glowing, and inspiring pæan of praise — a grand anthem to celebrate the glory, the mystery, and the majesty of Nature. It carries the reader back to the darkling woods which Boone saw in all their solitary and primeval splendor, when the fleet wild deer was his sacrifice, the mountain's crest his altar, and

> "Where erst, alone of all his race,
> He knelt to Nature's God."

No wonder that Byron, with all his genius, failed to come fully up to this subject. He only could do justice to "the brave old pioneer" who lived where he had lived ; who breathed the air that he had breathed ; whose eyes and soul had drunk in the natural beauties of Boone's old Kentucky home, and who had roamed amid the very scenes where once the war-whoop and the panther's scream had thrilled the old hunter's heart. It was left to O'Hara, who was born and reared in the home of Boone, to conceive the lofty imagery, and sing the tender and melancholy sentiment, of this poem. Need one apologise for the State pride which points to it as a poem peculiarly and absolutely Kentuckian ? The Marseillaise Hymn is not more distinctly a French production than is this poem a child of Kentucky. If it is true — as has been repeatedly asserted, and as this elegy strongly indicates — that the growth and quality of the literature of a people are largely influenced and dependent upon their natural surroundings, may we not reasonably hope much from the future

of a State so blessed in physical charms and character-
istics as the "Dark and Bloody Ground"?   Who will say
that the free, fresh air, the rugged scenery, and the inspiring associations of old Scotia had nothing to do with the
development of the genius of Sir Walter Scott?   Could
Rob Roy and the *Heart of Mid Lothian*, could *Marmion*
and the *Lay of the Last Minstrel* ever have been written
but by a native and lover of the land they depicted?   No :
their author could only have been one who had roamed
her lonely moors and trod her fragrant heather ; who loved
her gray old rocks and beetling crags ; who had heard the
roar of the cataract in her romantic glens and the scream
of the eagle in her mountain fastnesses, and whose soul
had been stirred by the weird music of the moaning pines
that stand like sentinels upon the shores of her beautiful
lakes.   If scenes like these foster and develop genius, then
we can understand one at least of the elements that have
entered into the creation of the orators and soldiers of
this most picturesque old Commonwealth, and we may

reasonably expect her to be the cradle of illustrious poets also. The Highlands of Scotland are not more wildly beautiful than the mountain regions of Kentucky. Her Blue Grass lands are as lovely and more fertile than the Campagna of Italy. Her forests in autumn are galleries of Nature's own most glorious handiwork. The sublimity of her vast, silent, and awe-inspiring caves is recognised the wide world over ; and that most picturesque of rivers, the Kentucky, with its towering cliffs and wooded heights, its rugged bed, shadowy shores, and miniature cascades, and its bold and hoary old rocks, crowned with feathery ferns, decked with beautiful mosses, and wrapped in fantastic vines, needs but ruined castles and crumbling battlements to make it far outvie the vaunted river Rhine. It was amid these triumphs of Nature's power that Theodore O'Hara was born ; at the shrine of Kentucky scenery he worshipped like an Eastern idolater, and his ode to Boone was the natural result. It is more — it is a prophecy of Kentucky's literary future ; and O'Hara is the forerunner of a line of poets who are destined to shed unfading lustre upon her.

Theodore O'Hara sleeps his last sleep by the side of his old comrades, under the shadow of the monument erected in their honor, and amid the scenes consecrated by his genius. It is well: for that beautiful spot was his favorite haunt, he loved its soothing solitude; it was there that the harp-strings of his soul first gave forth their sad but immortal notes, and it seems fitted by Nature for a poet's tomb. In death as in life, he seems the twin brother of Gray, the author of that exquisite emanation, the "Elegy in a Country Churchyard." Both were elegiac poets of wonderfully similar attainments and habits; both established their fame upon two or three short but finished productions, and both sleep at last amid the scenes and near the objects clothed with the glory of their inspiration. Gray slumbers in sight of the "antique towers" of Eton College, whose praises he sung, and in that churchyard where oft "the curfew tolled the knell of parting day."

O'Hara reposes in sight of the tomb of the "brave old
Pioneer" whose deathless dirge he sung, and in that cemetery where sleep the warriors whose requiem he chaunted,
and where

> "Glory guards with solemn round
> The bivouac of the dead."